Self-Portrait. 1514.
Drawing.
Biblio reale, Turin.
Art Resource

Leonardo da Vinci was born in the small Italian town of Vinci in 1452. He kept the name of his town for his own last name.

When he was little, Leonardo drew
pictures of plants, insects, flowers,
animals, and birds. He drew what he
saw in the countryside near his
home.

Leonardo da Vinci lived during a

time when people all over Europe were becoming interested in art. They wanted their cities, houses, and churches to be filled with beautiful statues and paintings. This period of time was called the Renaissance.

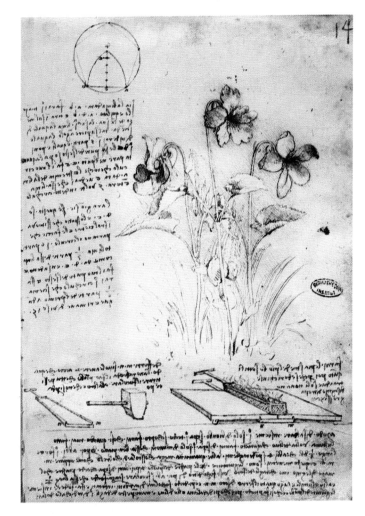

Botanical study. 1505. Drawing.
Bibliothéque de Institut de France, Paris.
Giraudon/Art Resource

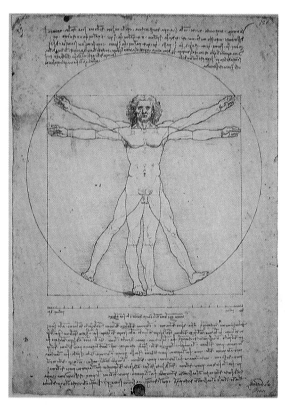

Human proportions reconstructed
according to Vitruvius.
1487-90 Drawing. Accademia, Venice.
Scala/Art Resource

Leonardo was a great artist, but he became famous because he was able to do so many other things, too. He was an architect, a musician, sculptor, scientist, inventor, and

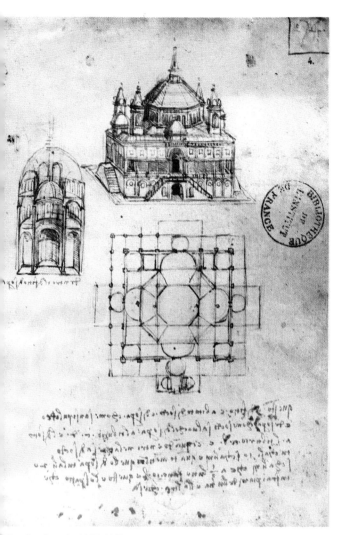

Plan for church. 1487-89 Drawing.
Bibliothéque de Institut de France, Paris
Giraudon/Art Resource

Plan of ideal city.
1487-89 Drawing.
Bibliothéque de Institut de France, Paris
Giraudon/Art Resource

mathematician. Leonardo designed
plans for beautiful churches, bridges,
even whole cities. He used his
drawings to help him see how things
would work.

Leonardo made lots of notes with his drawings. The unusual thing about the notes was, they were all written backwards!

To read Leonardo's notes, you would have to hold them up to a mirror. He probably didn't want people to read about his discoveries or steal his secrets.

The Annunication. 1472. Tempera and oil on wood. Uffizi, Florence. Scala/Art Resource

Leonardo used what he learned from nature and science to make his paintings look real.

In this painting, he made the angel wings from the things he had learned about bird wings. Leonardo knew how to paint beautiful plants, trees, and mountains, too.

When he was a teenager, Leonardo's father took him to

Baptism of Christ.
Andrea del Verrocchio.
1472. Oil.
Uffizi Gallery, Florence.
Scala/Art Resource

Florence, Italy, to learn about being
an artist at the workshop of the
famous Andrea del Verrocchio.
Florence was one of the greatest art
cities in Europe.

When he was twenty years old,
Leonardo helped his teacher finish
this painting. Leonardo painted the
angel kneeling in the lower corner.

Many people in Florence thought Leonardo's angel was the best part of the picture because it looked much more like a living angel than the other stiff-looking figures.

It wasn't long before Leonardo was asked to do whole paintings by himself.

Detail of *Baptism of Christ*.

Ginevra de'Benci. 1474. Tempera on wood.
National Gallery of Art, Washington, D.C.

Leonardo painted beautiful
portraits. In this picture, he used
what he had learned about nature
and science to make the background
as realistic as the lady. Leonardo
made this painting so smooth you
can hardly see a brush mark.

La Madonna Benois.
1478.
Tempera on wood.
Hermitage Museum,
Leningrad.
Scala/Art Resource

Leonardo was one of the first
artists to paint the mother of Jesus
smiling and playing with her baby.
Before this, artists showed Jesus and
his mother looking very serious.

St. Jerome. 1481 Underpainting
Vatican Museum, Rome. Scala/Art Resource

The Adoration of the Magi.
1481-82 Underpainting. Uffizi, Florence.
Scala/Art Resource

Leonardo was asked to paint these two pictures, but he never finished them! Nobody knows why. He left other paintings unfinished, too. Maybe he got too busy with his experiments and inventions.

The people of Florence may have heard about Leonardo's unfinished paintings.

About 1482 Leonardo decided to leave Florence and go to another great art city, Milan.

The Virgin of the Rocks. 1488.
Tempera and oil on wood.
Louvre, Paris.
Scala/Art Resource

One of the first things Leonardo did when he got to Milan was paint *The Virgin of the Rocks.*

This painting was very important in the history of art. Before it was painted, most artists would outline their people and use very flat backgrounds. Leonardo painted his figures without outlining them.

He made the shadowy part of the people almost blend into the mysterious background. The parts of the people that have light on them seem to come forward and appear almost three-dimensional.

The Virgin of the Rocks. 1506.
Tempera on wood.
National Gallery, London.
Scala/Art Resource

A lot of people must have liked *The Virgin of the Rocks,* because a few years later Leonardo painted another one. They look almost exactly the same.

Look at how much more lifelike Leonardo's painting is than this painting, which was done about the same time by another artist.

Madonna and Child.
Filippino Lippi.
Tempera and oil
on wood.
Metropolitan Museum
of Art, New York

War Machine. 1485. Drawing. British Museum, London. Marburg/Art Resource

Before Leonardo moved to Milan, he promised the duke of Milan that he would make him war machines to protect the city against the duke's enemies.

This seemed like an unusual thing for Leonardo to do, because he was a very gentle person who hated war.

Leonardo made lots of drawings of these machines. Some of them seemed as if they would work, but some of them didn't look like they would work at all.

Armored Car.
1485. Drawing.
British Museum, London.
Marburg/Art Resource

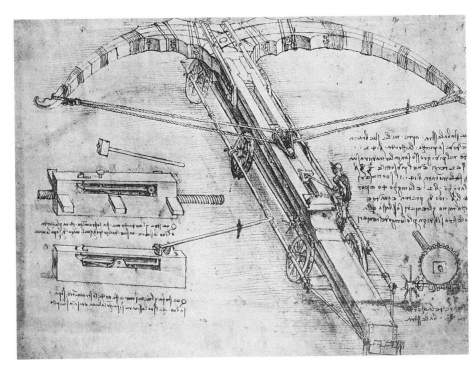

Giant Crossbow.
1489-90. Drawing.
Codex Atlanticus, Milan.
Art Resource

Gee, I wish that Leonardo guy was on our side.

THE LAST SUPPER

Leonardo da Vinci's greatest work was done for the wall of a dining room that was used by the monks at the Church of Santa Maria delle Grazie, in Milan.

The Last Supper shows Jesus with his closest friends, the twelve apostles.

Leonardo used all the things he had learned while doing his earlier paintings. The shadows, lighting, and background make this a beautiful painting.

The Last Supper. 1495-1497. Fresco. Santa Maria Delle Grazie, Milan. Scala/Art Resource

The special way Leonardo placed
the men around the table gives them
a feeling of movement that had never
been seen before.

Detail of *The Last Supper*

Today parts of *The Last Supper* are hard to see because the paint is chipping off. Leonardo was always experimenting with and making his own paint.

The paint he made for *The Last Supper* didn't work very well.

The Last Supper isn't the only painting that gave Leonardo problems. In one painting of a battle scene, the paint almost melted off the wall when Leonardo tried to dry it with fire pots.

The *Madonna and Child* looks all wrinkly because Leonardo may have mixed too much oil in the paint.

Detail of *Madonna and Child*. 1473. Tempera and oil on wood.
Alte Pinakothek, Munich. Scala/Art Resource

Some things that happened to Leonardo's paintings weren't his fault. It seems that people just couldn't keep their hands off his work.

The bottom of Ginevra de' Benci (on page 12) was cut off, and the painting of St. Jerome (page 14) was cut in half and used as a tabletop!

Someone even cut the sides off

Mona Lisa. 1503.
Tempera and oil on wood.
Louvre, Paris.
Giraudon/Art Resource

Leonardo's most famous painting, the *Mona Lisa.*

Ever since Leonardo painted the *Mona Lisa,* people have been talking about the mysterious look the lady has—especially her smile.

No matter where you stand, the *Mona Lisa* is always looking right into your eyes.

Detail of *Mona Lisa*.

The background of the *Mona Lisa* is very interesting, too. It looks like it's part of a science fiction or fairy-tale world. In a strange way, *Mona Lisa* and the background seem to blend together.

St. John the Baptist. 1515.
Tempera and oil on wood.
Louvre, Paris. Scala/Art Resource

St. Anne, Virgin and Child.
1500-1510. Tempera and oil on wood.
Louvre, Paris.
Scala/Art Resource

Leonardo painted only a few pictures after the *Mona Lisa*. He was more interested in working on his inventions and experiments. He spent the last years of his life in France, a guest of the King of France, making notes and drawings about his discoveries. He died there in 1519.

Leonardo da Vinci was one of the first artists to make his paintings seem real in all ways.

He gave the people in his paintings a feeling of movement and being alive.

Detail of *The Annunication* on page 9

Detail of *La Madonna Benois* on page 13

He used dark shadows and light colors to make what he was painting seem to come toward you and away from the painting.